MESOPOTAMIA

by Don Nardo

Content Adviser:
Anna Steinhelper, MA
PhD candidate and Development Administrator
Division of the Humanities
University of Chicago

COMPASS POINT BOOKS
a capstone imprint

Compass Point Books
1710 Roe Crest Drive
North Mankato, MN 56003
www.capstonepub.com

Managing Editor: Catherine Neitge
Designers: Heidi Thompson and Lori Bye
Media Researcher: Eric Gohl
Library Consultant: Kathleen Baxter
Production Specialist: Laura Manthe

Image Credits
Alamy: Mary Evans Picture Library, 35 (left), MiddleEast/Janzig, 24, National Geographic Image
Collection, 21; Art Resource, N.Y.: The Art Archive/Gianni Dagli Orti, 20, Balage Balogh, 30,
37, Erich Lessing, 7, The Metropolitan Museum of Art, 17; Corbis: Bettmann, 35 (right), 36,
Gianni Dagli Orti, 10, National Geographic Society, 19, 22, 31, PoodlesRock, 28; Getty Images:
AFP/Ali Al-Saadi, 42, AFP/Essam Al-Sudani, 8, The Bridgeman Art Library, 25, De Agostini/G.
Nimatallah/DEA, 16, Gamma-Keystone/Keystone-France, 40; iStockphoto: Floriano Rescigno,
cover (bottom left), Joel Carillet, 4, Paul Pantazescu, cover (bottom right), Steven Wynn, 29;
Newscom: akg-images, 13, 38, akg-images/Philippe Maillard, 26, 32, akg-images/Suzanne Held,
43, Robert Harding Productions, 39, World History Archive, 27; Shutterstock: Bond Girl, 12,
Brigida Soriano, 14, John Said, 11, Kamira, cover (top right), 9, 23, 33
Design Elements: Shutterstock: LeshaBu, MADDRAT, renew studio

Library of Congress Cataloging-in-Publication Data
Nardo, Don, 1947–
  Ancient Mesopotamia / by Don Nardo.
     p. cm.—(Exploring the ancient world)
  Includes bibliographical references and index.
  ISBN 978-0-7565-4567-3 (library binding)
  ISBN 978-0-7565-4588-8 (paperback)
  ISBN 978-0-7565-4628-1 (ebook PDF)
  1. Iraq—History—To 634—Juvenile literature. I. Title.
  DS71.N365 2013
  935—dc23   2012001988

Editor's Note: Compass Point Books uses new abbreviations to
distinguish time periods. For ancient times, instead of BC, we
use BCE, which means before the common era. BC means before
Christ. Similarly, we use CE, which means in the common era,
instead of AD. The abbreviation AD stands for the Latin phrase
anno Domini, which means in the year of our Lord, referring to Jesus Christ.

Printed in the United States of America in Stevens Point, Wisconsin.
032012   006678WZF12

Table of CONTENTS

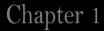
The Story of
MESOPOTAMIA

The great valley of the Tigris and Euphrates rivers witnessed the dawn of civilization. The peoples of ancient Mesopotamia were some of history's first farmers. They were also residents of the world's first cities and empires.

Their arts and crafts, and their political, military, and religious ideas have been passed down through the ages. A fair amount of what we do, say, and think today can be traced to what the Mesopotamians did, said, and thought.

The ruins of Sumerian, Babylonian, Assyrian, and Persian cities can still be seen in Iraq. They stand as mute witnesses to the region's amazing past, which gave humanity the gift of civilization and forever changed the world.

There was never a nation called Mesopotamia, but, rather, a large region in the middle of the Middle East. That region included much of what today is the country of Iraq. The name Mesopotamia came from Greek words meaning "between the rivers." Those rivers were the mighty Tigris and Euphrates. They flow roughly from northwest to southeast through the area. A large portion of Mesopotamia was a giant river valley. In the southeastern section of the valley were stretches of green farmlands and marshes. They were part of the vast deltas of the rivers, where they emptied into the Persian Gulf.

The fertile lower sector of Mesopotamia was called Sumer in early ancient times. It was the homeland of the first people to build a major civilization in the area—the Sumerians. After the Sumerian civilization declined, the area was usually called Babylonia. That name came from Babylon, the largest city that arose in southern Mesopotamia.

Moving toward the northwest, Mesopotamia's wetter region gave way to vast open plains. They were flat near the rivers, but

The historically important Euphrates River is the longest river in western Asia. It originates in Turkey and flows through Syria and Iraq.

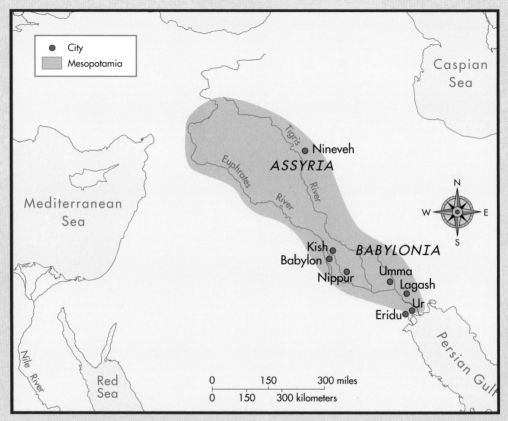

Ancient cities thrived along the Tigris and Euphrates rivers.

hillier in other places. The plains region of upper Mesopotamia was first called Akkad. Later people called it Assyria, after the Assyrians, a warlike people who ruled it for centuries. Later still both upper and lower Mesopotamia became part of the enormous Persian Empire.

The Sumerians, Babylonians, Assyrians, Persians, and several other peoples lived in Mesopotamia at various times from about 4000 BCE to 300 BCE. They were not the first residents of the region. That distinction belongs to small, unnamed groups that arrived dozens of centuries before.

These earliest peoples lived in an area that modern historians call the Fertile Crescent. It was a narrow strip of land lying along the western and northern borders of the Mesopotamian plains, stretching from the Persian Gulf in an arc to what is now Egypt. The Crescent's forested hills and valleys were well-watered and had excellent soil. So it is perhaps not surprising that some of the first known farmers in history settled in the Fertile Crescent. No one knows exactly when this pivotal event—the shift from hunter-gatherers to farmers—occurred. But experts think it was between 12,000 and 11,000 years ago.

Growing crops provided a permanent, secure food supply. So the early farmers, who had earlier been nomads, settled down. They built small villages and learned to make crude pottery and other craft items. They were so successful in their new lives that over time their numbers grew. Possibly because of population pressures in the Fertile Crescent, some of the inhabitants eventually decided to move. At some point between 6000 and 5000 BCE, they migrated onto the Mesopotamian plains.

The early Mesopotamians built

A man tends to a small plant next to a palm tree in a 5,000-year-old Sumerian carving.

villages and planted fields. They quickly learned that they had a major advantage over their ancestors in the Crescent. The advantage was the Tigris and Euphrates rivers. They could provide much more water for irrigating crops than the streams to the north and west. The farmers learned to dig long ditches from the rivers to their fields. With the irrigation canals, farmers could greatly expand their fields, which let them grow more crops.

The extra food supplies stimulated still more population growth. As a result, some of the villages grew into towns with populations of a few thousand people. Among the earliest thriving towns was Tepe Gawra, in northern Mesopotamia. Early towns that appeared to the south, near the Persian Gulf, included Ur, Eridu, and Uruk.

It was around the southern towns that the first of Mesopotamia's high cultures—the Sumerian—arose. Modern scholars are still unsure of the Sumerians' origins. They may have been people already living in the area. Or they may have been

Remains of the ancient Sumerian city of Uruk, which at one time was probably the largest city in the world

foreigners who entered the area from somewhere to the east.

Wherever they came from, the Sumerians were thriving by the early 3000s BCE. In the centuries that followed, they introduced important elements of civilization to the world. First they expanded some of their towns into cities. Some cities came to support populations in the tens of thousands. It would be more accurate to call them city-states. Each consisted of a central urban sector surrounded by villages and a large expanse of farmland and irrigation canals.

A high defensive wall made of dried mud-bricks typically protected a city-state's urban area. This was necessary because the city-states often attacked one another. Ruled by a king, each viewed itself as an independent nation and fiercely advanced its interests and influence. During periods of peace, the states eagerly traded foodstuffs, craft items, cloth, and other goods.

Another important advance the Sumerians made was the invention of writing. Between 3500 and 3000 BCE, a complex writing method developed in southern Mesopotamia. Tablets written in the Sumerian language have been found in many parts of southern Mesopotamia, with some of the earliest discovered in the city of Uruk. Scribes, men who were trained to read and write, pressed pointed sticks into moist clay tablets. Modern scholars call these wedge-shaped

A tablet covered with Sumerian writing

marks cuneiform. When dry, the tablets became the earliest examples of documents and letters.

While scribes kept busy producing tablets, battles and wars among the Sumerian states continued. Eventually one state conquered all the others. The king who created this empire— the world's first—was Sargon of Akkad, a town north of Babylonia. He reigned from about 2340 to 2284 BCE. During those years he and his forces overran not only southern Mesopotamia, but also much of the northern plains.

Sargon's large realm lasted about 150 years before other ambitious rulers in the region defeated it and created their own empires. In time the residents of the captured cities no longer thought of themselves as

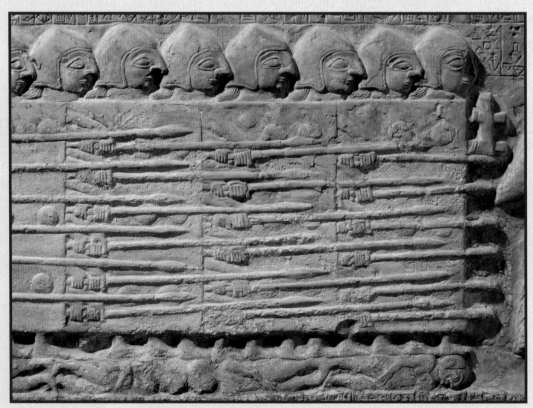

A 4,500-year-old plaque depicts Sumerian warriors trampling their enemies.

Sumerians. The Sumerian language ceased to be spoken on a daily basis. Still, Sumerian culture, including its gods and writing system, survived because later Mesopotamians adopted it.

Among the most successful of the later peoples were the inhabitants of the growing city of Babylon. Their ruler, Hammurabi, who ascended the throne in 1792 BCE, carved out an empire roughly as big as Sargon's. Babylon became the most splendid, envied city in Mesopotamia. Several peoples, some from the region and others from what are now Turkey and Iran, tried to capture it.

Only a few of Babylon's rivals managed to seize it. One was a formidable power that arose in upper Mesopotamia in the 1300s BCE—the fierce Assyrians. After their civilization rapidly expanded, one of their strongest kings, Tukulti-Ninurta I, triumphantly led them into Babylon sometime in the 1230s BCE.

The Assyrians were soon on the brink of conquering all of Mesopotamia, along with Syria and Palestine, on its western flank. But in the 1100s BCE much of the Middle East suffered a period of decline. Invaders who today are called the Sea Peoples swept through Egypt, Palestine, and parts of eastern Mesopotamia. They burned and looted many cities.

When the region began to recover in the 900s BCE, the

Assyrian soldiers struck fear throughout the Middle East.

Assyrians made a bold comeback. In the two centuries that followed, they built the biggest and most feared empire the world had yet seen. Particularly successful were the members of the Sargonid dynasty. Its founder, Sargon II, who reigned from 721 to 705 BCE, and his three successors were ruthless conquerors. They added Egypt to their growing empire before an alliance of opponents stopped them in 609 BCE.

One of the partners who brought down Assyria was a newly revived Babylon. The other was the Medes, a people from what is now western Iran. Both lorded over short-term empires in the region before another Iranian power arose and defeated them. That power was the Persian Empire, established by a dynamic, highly effective ruler— Cyrus II—in 559 BCE.

Cyrus and his immediate successors created what was then the largest empire in the world. It stretched from the shores of the Mediterranean Sea in the west to the borders

A carving from Sargon II's palace

Babylon at Its Height

After the final defeat of Assyria in 609 BCE, the victorious Babylonians ruled large parts of Mesopotamia. Among other things, they renovated and expanded Babylon, raising it to new heights of splendor. The greatest Babylonian king of the age, Nebuchadnezzar II, who reigned ca. 605– 562 BCE, built new temples, canals, and palaces. Tradition says he erected the famous Hanging Gardens of Babylon, a gift for one of his wives. A huge structure covered with trees and flowers, it was later listed as one of the Seven Wonders of the Ancient World.

The legendary Hanging Gardens of Babylon

of India in the east. Dozens of peoples, speaking many languages, did the bidding of the mighty Persian monarchs.

Yet as had happened so often in the past, this great power had its moment in the sun and then declined. The relentless cycle of conquest, empire, and decline, followed by new conquest, continued in Mesopotamia. The Greeks, led by Alexander the Great, overran the Persian realm in the 330s and 320s BCE. This began almost two centuries of Greek rule in the region.

The Greeks, in their turn, were driven out by another Iranian people, the Parthians. The Parthians ruled Mesopotamia until 224 CE, when the Sassanians took charge

Alexander the Great's victories began nearly 200 years of Greek rule in Mesopotamia.

and revived many Persian customs, institutions, and beliefs.

Finally, in 651 an Arab Muslim army swept onto the Mesopotamian plains. That event marked the close of the region's ancient era. Thereafter, a long series of Muslim peoples and empires held sway in the great valley of the Tigris and Euphrates.

Peoples Who Ruled Mesopotamia

People	Rule Began	Notable Rulers
Sumerians	3000s BCE	Gilgamesh, Sargon, Gudea
Babylonians	1700s BCE	Hammurabi
Assyrians	1300s BCE	Ashur-uballit I, Tukulti-Ninurta I, Tiglathpileser I, Sargon II
Babylonians	600s BCE	Nebuchadnezzar II
Persians	500s BCE	Cyrus II, Darius I, Xerxes I
Greeks	300s BCE	Alexander III ("the Great"), Seleucus I, Antiochus III
Parthians	100s BCE	Arsaces, Mithridates I
Sassanians	200s CE	Ardashir, Shapur I
Arabs	600s CE	Umar, Uthman

Chapter 2

Family and
Home Life

Few written records of the everyday lives of ordinary Sumerians, Babylonians, Assyrians, and other Mesopotamians has been found. Luckily, however, archaeologists have unearthed a wide array of artifacts from ruined cities in the region. Such artifacts include pottery, jewelry, and cooking pots and utensils. Pieces of furniture, scraps of clothing, figurines, and the foundations of houses have also been found. Combining this evidence with the limited written

records has allowed scholars to piece together a rough picture of family life in the region in ancient times.

That picture shows that nearly all families were patriarchal—male-dominated. They were also patrilineal, which means that land, houses, and other family property passed from a father to his sons when he died. Women almost never inherited property. But if a father approved, a daughter who had no brothers could receive a legacy.

The inherited property included more than land, a house, furniture, and animals. Any slaves the family owned also passed from father to child. The average Mesopotamian family owned two to four slaves. In contrast, wealthy households kept 40 or more slaves. Palaces and temples sometimes had hundreds.

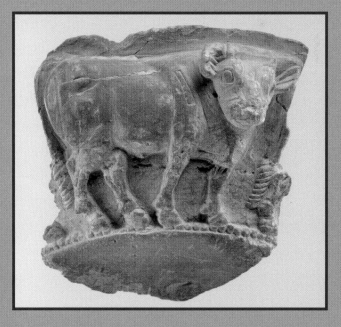

A relief of slaves hauling buiding materials (left) and a bowl carved with bulls (above) give historians glimpses of life in ancient Mesopotamia.

The fact that women usually did not inherit property shows that they had fewer rights than men. A wife remained under her husband's control throughout their marriage. Like her daughters and the family slaves, she was also expected to follow the orders of the man of the house. A daughter remained obedient to her father until she got married. At that point, her husband replaced her father as her master.

Mesopotamian women did have one important right. They were allowed to work outside the home, which gave them a fair degree of freedom during much of an average day. Moreover, evidence indicates that in the early 1000s BCE some women in Babylon did jobs most often performed by men. There were a few female scribes, artists, and doctors, for example.

Most women, however, especially in the lower classes, did work requiring less skill. In the countryside some helped their husbands and brothers plant and harvest crops and care for farm animals. In the towns, making cloth was a common task for women.

Whether or not she had a job, the average Mesopotamian woman was expected to perform certain duties in the home. These included raising the children, cooking, and cleaning. By contrast, a handful of very rich and royal women did not have to work at all. These high-status women had personal servants and enjoyed fine clothes, expensive perfumes, and other luxuries. Particularly respected and well-treated were priestesses, who led prayers in temples. Most priestesses were not allowed to marry and have children. But they could own and manage land and other property.

Most Mesopotamian women—unlike priestesses—were expected to marry and have children. In a few cases, the bride and groom may have been in love. But almost all marriages were arranged. The fathers or grandfathers of the young man and woman made a deal and even signed a contract.

A bride's father sealed a marriage contract as the couple watched.

Also, the groom, or his father or uncle, spoke with the bride's father about the dowry. This consisted of money or valuable goods that the bride's father gave the groom.

After the marriage was arranged, the wedding took place. It was not a ceremony, but instead a big feast arranged by the groom's father. Members of both families mingled, made speeches, and got to know one another. After the wedding feast, the bride and groom were considered married.

As happens today, some marriages in Mesopotamia did not work out. Divorce was allowed in some cases, such as when a husband beat his wife. If she could show proof of the abuse, a divorce was granted. If a wife could not bear children, her husband might request a divorce. Divorced women usually kept their dowries.

Whether the children of a divorced couple ended up with the father or the mother depended on the individual situation, as is the case today. Babylonian laws controlled what happened to the children. This was because the welfare of children was seen as vital to society's future.

Very little is known about how children were raised in ancient Mesopotamia. Evidence does show that they played with toys. Boys had miniature chariots and slingshots, while girls had dolls and miniature furniture. Children of both sexes played with jump ropes, balls, and hoops.

If a married couple could not have children, it was common to adopt one or more. One form of adoption consisted of rescuing a baby who had been abandoned. Another common situation was when a father and mother could not afford to feed and clothe all their children. They made a deal to give a child to a couple seeking to adopt.

Such cases were undoubtedly sad for the couple and child who parted ways. Yet for the adoptive parents such a deal might well save their family line from dying out. This was essential in a culture that distrusted change and felt that family and social traditions must be carried on.

An ancient relief of women among date palms

Humanity's First Schools

Ancient Mesopotamia was the site of the world's first known formal schools. In the ruins of the Sumerian city Uruk, archaeologists have found lists of vocabulary words used by students. The lists date to as early as 3000 BCE. Also, the physical remains of schools have come to light in Uruk, as well as in Ur, Mari, and other Mesopotamian cities.

The school in Mari had two rooms. One featured benches on which up to four students sat. They used wooden writing boards covered with wax. A child made letters and words by moving a pointed stick across the wax. Later the wax would be smoothed to make a fresh surface.

Only boys attended school in ancient Mesopotamia.

Chapter 3

Arts and Architecture

The peoples of ancient Mesopotamia produced a great deal of noteworthy art, including monumental architecture. But nearly nothing is known about the artists themselves. This is because they mostly belonged to society's lower classes. In those days writers rarely described the lives of the poor and less privileged. They concentrated on the well-to-do and the nobility, for which most of the art was created. For example, most of the

statues and other large sculptures carved by Mesopotamian artists were intended for palaces or temples.

All of the region's peoples produced such sculptures. But perhaps the largest and most striking examples were those made by the Assyrians nearly 3,000 years ago. The statues they turned out mainly were of kings, gods, animals, and mythical beings. Bulls were particularly popular subjects. The biggest examples were human-headed, winged bulls that guarded the entrances to the Assyrian palaces. They were known as *lamassu*, meaning "bull men." Surviving examples weigh close to 20 tons (18 metric tons).

Assyrian and other Mesopotamian sculptors also created bas-reliefs. They are carved scenes raised slightly from flat surfaces, usually walls, but also doors, pillars, and other objects. Several Assyrian monarchs ordered the creation of long panels of relief sculptures on the walls of their palaces. They portray military victories and other major accomplishments of the kings. Such reliefs were not meant solely as decorative art. They were also a kind of propaganda designed to impress both the Assyrian people and foreign visitors.

A giant guardian sculpture (left) was hauled into place. Warriors (above right) were the focal point of an ancient bas-relief.

The Imposing Behistun Rock

The Assyrians were not the only Mesopotamians who created impressive sculptures. Among the many produced later by the Persians were large reliefs carved onto the faces of rocks and cliffs. Especially imposing is the Behistun Rock, a giant rock face along the road to Babylon in what is now western Iran. In the sculpted scene towers Persia's King Darius I, who ruled from about 522 to 486 BCE. Next to him are 10 of his conquered enemies, tied by ropes. Text sculpted in three languages tells of Darius' reign.

The Behistun Rock's text helped unlock the secrets of ancient cuneiform writing.

Ancient Mesopotamian artists also produced many beautiful painted wall murals in palaces, temples, and homes of the wealthy. Of the murals that have survived, some of the best preserved come from Mari, an ancient city that was close to the Euphrates River in western Mesopotamia. The dozens of detailed murals were done for the palace of King Zimri-Lim, who reigned from about 1775 to 1761 BCE. One depicts the ruler swearing an oath to the goddess Ishtar, who was thought to protect kings.

The first step in making such a mural was to coat the wall with a layer of plaster. When it dried, the artist sketched the outlines of the picture and then applied his paint. In the late 1000s BCE, this method of painting on a dry surface was replaced by the fresco technique. A fresco is a painting done on wet plaster. The main advantage is that the paint and plaster dry together, making the colors last longer.

The pigments of the paints used by Mesopotamian artists came mostly from minerals. Red, for instance, was made from iron oxide, and black pigment came from soot or tar. Green paint was made from malachite, a greenish substance found in copper ores. A painter mixed these pigments with egg whites or milk solids to create the paint.

A priest leads a bull to sacrifice in a mural at the palace of King Zimri-Lim.

Cylinder Seal

A special form of ancient art from Mesopotamia is today called a cylinder seal. It is a small piece of stone, or less often glass, ivory, shell, copper, or bronze. On it an artist known as a seal-cutter carved a tiny picture or a written message. The seal could then be pressed into moist clay, creating an imprint, which identified a person, family, or social institution. Millions of cylinder seals were made over the centuries by the various Mesopotamian peoples. Several of these have been unearthed and can be seen in museums across the world.

A 4,000-year-old lapis lazuli cylinder seal

Everyday activities were depicted on one side of the Standard of Ur.

Other delicate decorative artworks produced in ancient Mesopotamia were mosaics. A mosaic is an artistic image created by gluing many small colored tiles, stones, pieces of glass, or other objects to a floor, wall, or other surface.

The finest early example of a mosaic from the region is the famous Standard of Ur. Experts estimate that this Sumerian artifact was made sometime in the mid-2000s BCE.

The scenes are made up of many tiny pieces of shell, red limestone, and a blue stone called lapis lazuli. One scene depicts a Sumerian military battle. Another shows a grand celebration staged by the victors, including a banquet and a parade. The Standard is more than just a beautiful piece of art. It is important to historians because it shows how the Sumerians lived and dressed.

The largest examples of art

A ziggurat loomed in the ancient Assyrian capital of Nineveh.

from ancient Mesopotamia are its palaces, temples, and other important buildings. The biggest and most awe-inspiring structures were ziggurats, which were unique to the region. Ziggurats are gigantic pyramid-like structures with stepped platforms that were used for religious purposes. Each ziggurat had a large stairway or ramp. Priests climbed the stairs to reach a small chapel at the summit.

Ziggurats and other large Mesopotamian structures were composed of huge numbers of clay bricks. This was because the region had few forests to supply wood and very little native stone. Builders sometimes mixed reed matting or rope with the clay to give it extra strength. Even so, rain, wind, and sun caused the bricks to crumble fairly quickly. So such buildings required frequent repairs. Centuries later, when the Mesopotamian cities were abandoned, the bricks fell apart, creating large mounds of debris called tells. The tells barely hint at the region's former artistic splendor.

Musicians and Songs

The people of ancient Mesopotamia enjoyed music no less than people do today. Music played a central role in religious festivals, meetings of the royal court, and other community activities. Among the songs were hymns to the gods and kings, expressions of grief for dead kings, marching music for soldiers, and tunes to celebrate weddings and homecomings. The instruments the musicians played included drums, cymbals, tambourines, harps, whistles, and pipes like modern flutes and oboes.

A vintage engraving reproduces a bas-relief of harp players discovered in Nineveh.

Chapter 4

Gods and Religious Beliefs

Like all ancient peoples, those who lived in ancient Mesopotamia were devoutly religious. They believed that many kinds of invisible gods and spirits dwelled within nature. The sky, moon, planets, rivers, seas, forests, hills, and even farm fields—all were seen to be inhabited by beings more powerful than humans.

People believed that the gods guided or influenced the deeds and fates of humans. Heavenly forces might decide who won or lost a battle, for instance. Similarly, people often looked to the gods to overcome sickness, end a drought, or bring good fortune.

Such divine guidance and favors did not come free, however. The gods expected, even demanded, some things in return. One was to follow basic social rules the deities had established. The Sumerians called these rules *me*. In the language spoken by the Babylonians and Assyrians, they were known as *parsu*. The rules included telling the truth, behaving in a civilized manner, and seeking justice. Also, the gods expected kings to make constructive laws and their subjects to obey them.

The main entrance to Babylon (left), a giant blue gate, was dedicated to the goddess Ishtar. Mesopotamian temples (above) dwarfed the people entering them.

Another way that humans appeased the gods was through rituals of worship. One of the two most common rituals was prayer. Another was making offerings to the gods. The offerings usually were edible substances intended to nourish the gods. Oils and butter were common, as were sacrificed animals, including cattle, sheep, and goats.

Besides formal offerings made at public altars, offering ceremonies took place inside temples. There priests provided meals for one or more gods every day. Built to honor the gods, temples were another important aspect of religious beliefs and worship. As a rule, ordinary people did not worship inside a temple. This was because it was thought that the god lived there, within his or her statue. To respect the deity's privacy, only priests and kings were allowed inside the sacred chambers.

Still another way that people appeased and honored the gods was by taking part in religious festivals. The biggest was a celebration of fertile soil and growing crops.

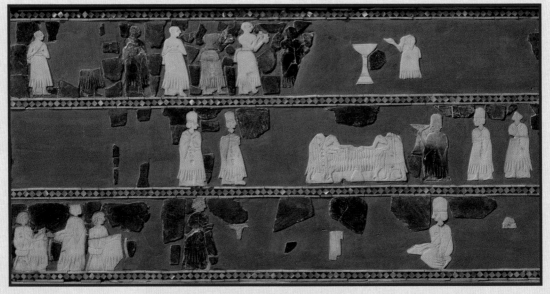

An ancient Sumerian temple depiction of a procession of women and priests during an animal sacrifice

The Sumerians called the festival Akiti, and the Babylonians and Assyrians called it Akitu. Usually it was held every March at harvest time. The Mesopotamian New Year also took place in March, so many people eagerly and loudly celebrated both traditions at the same time. The Babylonian version of the holiday lasted 12 days. People prayed, sacrificed animals, carried images of gods through the streets, sang songs, and feasted.

Most of the deities honored in these festivities were originally part of the Sumerian pantheon, the group of all gods. As each new national group rose to prominence in the region, it tended to adopt the same gods. Or it associated a leading Sumerian god with a deity of its own that had similar traits. When an older god was borrowed, his or her name frequently was changed. In this way, the chief Sumerian deity, Enlil, was worshipped by the Babylonians as Marduk. The Assyrians called the same god Ashur.

The eagle-faced god Ashur

The Major Sumerian Gods

Name	Role	Babylonian Equivalent
Enlil	Leader of the gods	Marduk
Enki	God of fresh water, wisdom, and fertility	Ea
An	God of the heavens and father of Enlil	Anu
Inanna	Goddess of love	Ishtar
Utu	God of the sun	Shamash
Nanna	God of the moon	Sin
Ninhursag	Mother figure and creator deity	Aruru
Ereshkigal	Queen of the Underworld	Ereshkigal
Nergal	King of the Underworld and god of war	Erra

Inanna, also known as Ishtar

Enlil, also known as Marduk

The king of the ancient city of Ur makes an offering to Nanna, the moon god, in a 4,000-year-old bas-relief discovered in 1925.

It was thought that Enlil viewed a few people as special and decided that they should serve as kings over their fellow humans. He also made sure that crops would grow by bringing rain and promoting the richness of the soil. But Enlil also could use rain to punish people, as in the case of disastrous floods.

Among the other prominent Mesopotamian deities was Enlil's son, Utu, god of the sun, who brought light and warmth. The Babylonians and Assyrians called him Shamash. Two of Enlil's other children were also very important in the region's religious worship and lore. They were the moon god Nanna and Inanna, goddess of love and war. Later Mesopotamians called Inanna

Ishtar, and people in Syria, Palestine, and Egypt recognized her as Astarte. Later still and to the west, the Greeks adopted her as Aphrodite and the Romans as Venus.

No less important was the Sumerian god Enki, who was known as Ea to the Babylonians. He was the deity of flowing waters. Artists often showed the life-giving Tigris and Euphrates rivers gushing from his massive body. Enki was also the wisest of the Mesopotamian gods. It was said that he harbored secret knowledge of magic as well, making him a mysterious figure.

People in the vast Tigris and Euphrates valley worshipped these and other gods regularly. Yet most Mesopotamians did not do so only because they feared divine wrath. Their devotion to religion came also from a strong sense of morality that they believed the gods demanded

The god Enki was said to have lived in the ancient Sumerian city of Eridu. An artist depicts him sailing to the Underworld.

of them. The Sumerians deeply admired truth, justice, freedom, and human compassion. At the same time, they hated dishonesty, unfairness, and cruelty. These principles stemmed mainly from the religious faith they acquired beginning when they were small children. Indeed, in Sumerian hymns the gods were constantly praised for being champions of truth and goodness.

Like all human societies, those of the Sumerians and their descendants must have had their share of deceit, disorder, and crime. Thanks to religion, the negative forces were held in check by a much stronger positive force. It was a powerful sense of right and wrong enforced by the majority in society. The Sumerians had a word for their feeling of respect for their fellow humans—*namlulu*. Moreover, they often acted on it by protecting the weakest among them and upholding justice and fair dealings. Over time, such ethical

A water-giving goddess adorned a temple honoring Inanna built in about 1410 BCE.

behavior was set in stone, so to speak, in the world's first written laws. In this way, Mesopotamian religious devotion helped to set much of humankind on a path toward higher civilization.

Persian Religious Beliefs

The Babylonians and Assyrians carried on the religious traditions of the Sumerians. In the 500s BCE, however, the Persians introduced a new faith into Mesopotamia. It was based on the teachings of an Iranian prophet named Zarathustra. The Greeks called him Zoroaster, by which he is better known today. He maintained that an Iranian sky deity named Ahura-Mazda was the main god of the universe. The virtuous Ahura-Mazda was locked in an eternal struggle against evil.

Followers of Zoroastrianism were expected to reject the evil. They were also encouraged to do good deeds, think good thoughts, and aid the poor and oppressed. About 200,000 people follow the faith today in the Middle East, India, and elsewhere.

In a relief he had carved, Persian King Ardashir I receives a ring from Ahura-Mazda (right) showing the god's approval of his reign (226–242).

Chapter 5

A Profound
Legacy

Iraq—the site of ancient Mesopotamia—officially became a nation in the 1930s. At the time, like many other Middle Eastern countries, it was poor and its people had few machines and other advances. People living in Western nations looked on the area as backward and unimportant.

In part this was because many aspects of everyday life in the former Mesopotamia had undergone little or no change since ancient times. A striking example was a typical street market. After excavating ancient Sumerian and Babylonian markets, archaeologists noticed something remarkable. The ancient markets were nearly identical to modern Iraqi ones. Both were filled with makeshift merchants' booths with cloth awnings to shield people from the hot sun. The old and new versions alike lacked electricity, running water, and other conveniences.

In addition, early modern Iraqi city dwellers lived in houses much like the small mud-brick ones of their ancient ancestors. The same was true of the inhabitants of the broad marshes stretching across sections of southern Iraq. The ancient marsh dwellers built their houses from the reeds that grow in the Tigris and Euphrates rivers. As late as the 1970s, many rural Iraqis erected identical reed huts. Also like their ancient counterparts, the Iraqi marsh dwellers used small boats fashioned from reeds. Similarly, the men and boys still enjoyed a game that originated in Sumer nearly 60 centuries ago. The players stood in their boats and tried to push their opponents into the water.

The market in 1930s Baghdad, Iraq, had not changed much since ancient times.

An Iraqi woman makes a basket out of reeds, much as her ancestors did.

Well into the 20th century, Iraq was a place where past and present met daily. Its technology and living standards remained far behind those of Western nations. Few people in the West were aware of Iraq's glorious past. Nor did they appreciate the huge cultural debt they owed to the peoples and nations of ancient Mesopotamia.

Today the significance of that huge debt is better understood. It is widely known that some of the first forms of agriculture began in the hills overlooking the Mesopotamian plains. Later the first cities sprang up on those plains.

The first governments were

formed to run those cities. The cities were also where writing was invented and some of the first schools were established. Other firsts established by the Sumerians and their immediate successors are irrigation canals, roads, religious temples, written laws and courts, charts showing the stars and planets, and the concept of kings' receiving divine authority to rule.

These and other civilized advances steadily spread outward from ancient Mesopotamia to other parts of the globe. Peoples in India, Europe, and Africa felt their influence. They absorbed the ideas, making them their own. Then they passed them along to others. This slow but relentless process is called cultural diffusion. It continued through many centuries and countless generations until Mesopotamia's profound legacy reached the present day. In a surprising number of ways, it helped to make the author of this book, along with all of its readers, who we are.

A *lamassu* guards the entrance of the Gate of All Nations in Persepolis, Iran, built by King Xerxes in the 400s BCE.

Timeline

ca. 10,000–9000 BCE	Agriculture begins in the Fertile Crescent, along the western and northern edges of the Mesopotamian plains
ca. 6000–5000 BCE	People in the Fertile Crescent erect villages
ca. 3500–3000 BCE	The Sumerians begin building the world's first cities, where the first writing system develops
ca. 2340 to 2284 BCE	Sargon the Great, the king of Akkad, establishes and rules the world's first empire
ca. 1792 BCE	Hammurabi becomes king of Babylon; he carves out an empire and issues a set of laws that were of lasting importance
ca. 1775–1761 BCE	King Zimri-Lim rules the city-state of Mari, in western Mesopotamia
1300s BCE	The Assyrians rapidly expand their territory and create an empire in Mesopotamia
ca. 1200–1100 BCE	Invaders known as the Sea Peoples sweep through parts of the Middle East, including western Mesopotamia
ca. 721–705 BCE	Reign of Sargon II; under Sargon and his successors, the Assyrian Empire reaches its greatest size and power
609 BCE	Assyria falls to the Medes and Babylonians, who establish their own empires
605–562 BCE	King Nebuchadnezzar II of Babylonia expands Babylon and builds the famous Hanging Gardens there
559 BCE	Cyrus II becomes the first king of the Persian Empire
522–486 BCE	King Darius I expands the Persian realm, making it the largest empire the world had seen
334 BCE	Alexander the Great, the Macedonian Greek conqueror, attacks the Persian Empire; in less than a decade it falls to him
323 BCE	Alexander dies in Babylon, leaving his chief generals to fight for control of his empire
141 BCE	An Iranian people, the Parthians, seize control of Mesopotamia from the Greeks
224 CE	The Sassanians defeat the Parthians and begin to revive Persian customs in Mesopotamia
651 CE	Most of Mesopotamia falls to Muslim Arab armies

Glossary

bas-relief—carved scene raised slightly from a flat surface

cultural diffusion—process in which ideas and customs spread from one people and place to another over time

cuneiform—system of writing invented by the Sumerians; it used wedge-shaped characters

dowry—money or valuables that a bride's father gives to her husband in marriage

dynasty—succession of rulers from the same family

fresco—painting done on wet plaster

iron oxide—rust, which Mesopotamian painters used to make red paint

lapis lazuli—semiprecious stone with a bluish hue

mosaic—picture pieced together from many small tiles made of stone, shell, or other materials

nobility—class of people who have a high rank or title

nomads—people with no established home who move from place to place

pantheon—group of gods worshipped by a people or nation

patriarchal—describing a form of social organization in which the father is the highest authority in the family, clan, or tribe

patrilineal—system of inheritance in which land and other property pass from father to son

propaganda—information spread to influence the thinking of people; often not completely true or fair

scribe—in the ancient world, a person who made a living with his or her reading and writing skills

urban—having to do with a city

ziggurat—large, pyramid-like structure used for religious purposes in ancient Mesopotamia

Select Bibliography

Ascalone, Enrico. *Mesopotamia*. Berkeley: University of California Press, 2007.

Bahrani, Zainab. *Women of Babylon: Gender and Representation in Mesopotamia*. London: Routledge, 2001.

Bancroft-Hunt, Norman. *Historical Atlas of Ancient Mesopotamia*. New York: Checkmark Books, 2004.

Bertman, Stephen. *Handbook to Life in Ancient Mesopotamia*. New York: Facts on File, 2003.

Black, Jeremy, et al. *The Literature of Ancient Sumer*. New York: Oxford University Press, 2004.

Bottéro, Jean. *Religion in Ancient Mesopotamia*. Translated by Teresa L. Fagan. Chicago: University of Chicago Press, 2001.

Cartledge, Paul. *Alexander the Great: The Hunt for a New Past*. Woodstock, N.Y.: Overlook Press, 2004.

Casson, Lionel. *The Ancient Mariners: Seafarers and Sea Fighters of the Mediterranean in Ancient Times*. Princeton, N.J.: Princeton University Press, 1991.

Ceram, C.W., ed. *Hands on the Past: Pioneer Archaeologists Tell Their Own Story*. New York: Knopf, 1966.

Collon, Dominique. *Ancient Near Eastern Art*. Berkeley: University of California Press, 1995.

Cotterell, Arthur. *Chariot: From Chariot to Tank, the Astounding Rise and Fall of the World's First War Machine*. Woodstock, N.Y.: Overlook Press, 2005.

Crawford, Harriet E.W. *Sumer and the Sumerians*. Cambridge, U.K.: Cambridge University Press, 2004.

Curatola, Giovanni, et al. *The Art and Architecture of Mesopotamia*. New York: Abbeville Press, 2007.

Curtis, John, ed. *Later Mesopotamia and Iran: Tribes and Empires, 1600–539 B.C.: Proceedings of a Seminar in Memory of Vladimir G. Lukonin*. London: British Museum Press, 1995.

Dalley, Stephanie, trans. *Myths from Mesopotamia: Creation, the Flood, Gilgamesh, and Others*. New York: Oxford University Press, 1989.

Foster, Benjamin R., ed. *From Distant Days: Myths, Tales, and Poetry of Ancient Mesopotamia*. Bethesda, Md.: CDL Press, 1995.

Gershevitch, Ilya, ed. *The Cambridge History of Iran, Volume 2: The Median and Achaemenian Periods*. Cambridge, U.K.: Cambridge University Press, 1985.

Healy, Mark. *The Ancient Assyrians*. Oxford, U.K.: Osprey Publishing, 1991.

Kramer, Samuel N., and the editors of Time-Life Books. *Cradle of Civilization*. New York: Time Inc., 1967.

Kramer, Samuel N. *The Sumerians: Their History, Culture, and Character*. Chicago: University of Chicago Press, 1963.

Kuhrt, Amélie. *The Ancient Near East, vols. 1 and 2*. London: Routledge, 1995.

Layard, Austen Henry. *Nineveh and Its Remains: A Narrative of an Expedition to Assyria during the Years 1845, 1846 & 1847*. London: Murray, 1867.

Leick, Gwendolyn. *A Dictionary of Ancient Near Eastern Mythology*. London: Routledge, 1991.

Leick, Gwendolyn. *Mesopotamia: The Invention of the City*. London: Penguin, 2002.

Livius: Articles on Ancient History. 11 May 2012. www.livius.org

Lloyd, Seton. *The Archaeology of Mesopotamia: From the Old Stone Age to the Persian Conquest*. New York: Thames and Hudson, 1984.

Luckenbill, Daniel D., ed. *Ancient Records of Assyria and Babylonia*. 2 vols. Chicago: University of Chicago Press, 1926–27.

Mesopotamia—The British Museum. 30 April 2012. www.mesopotamia.co.uk/menu.html

Nemet-Nejat, Karen Rhea. *Daily Life in Ancient Mesopotamia*. Peabody, Mass.: Hendrickson Publishers, 2002.

Olmstead, A.T. *History of Assyria*. Chicago: University of Chicago Press, 1960.

The Oriental Institute of the University of Chicago. 30 April 2012. http://oi.uchicago.edu/

Pollock, Susan. *Ancient Mesopotamia: The Eden That Never Was*. Cambridge, U.K.: Cambridge University Press, 1999.

Postgate, J.N. *Early Mesopotamia: Society and Economy at the Dawn of History*. London: Routledge, 1992.

Pritchard, James B., ed. *The Ancient Near East: Supplementary Texts and Pictures Relating to the Old Testament*. Princeton, N.J.: Princeton University Press, 1969.

Roth, Martha Tobi. *Law Collections from Mesopotamia and Asia Minor*. Atlanta: Scholars Press, 1995.

Roux, Georges. *Ancient Iraq*. New York: Penguin, 1992.

Ryan, William B.F., and Walter C. Pitman. *Noah's Flood: The New Scientific Discoveries about the Event that Changed History*. New York: Simon and Schuster, 1998.

Saggs, H.W.F. *Babylonians*. Berkeley: University of California Press, 2000.

Saggs, H.W.F. *Civilization Before Greece and Rome*. New Haven: Yale University Press, 1989.

Saggs, H.W.F. *The Might that was Assyria*. London: Sidgwick and Jackson, 1984.

Sasson, Jack M., ed. *Civilizations of the Ancient Near East*. New York: Scribner, 1995.

Snell, Daniel C. *Life in the Ancient Near East, 3100–332 B.C.E.* New Haven: Yale University Press, 1997.

Veenhof, Klaas R., ed. *Houses and Households in Ancient Mesopotamia*. Istanbul, Turkey: Netherlands Historical-Archaeological Institute of Istanbul, 1996.

Further Reading

Burgan, Michael. *Empires of Ancient Persia.*
New York: Chelsea House, 2009.

Hunter, Erica C.D. *Ancient Mesopotamia: A Cultural Atlas for Young People.*
New York: Chelsea House, 2007.

Oakes, Lorna. *Mesopotamia.*
New York: Rosen Pub., 2009.

Rustad, Martha E.H. *The Babylonians: Life in Ancient Babylon.*
Minneapolis: Millbrook Press, 2010.

Stefoff, Rebecca. *The Ancient Near East.*
New York: Benchmark Books, 2005.

On the Web

Use FactHound to find Internet sites related to this book. All of the sites on FactHound have been researched by our staff.

Here's all you do:
Visit www.facthound.com
Type in this code: 9780756545673

Titles in this Series:

The Byzantine Empire
Ancient China
Ancient Egypt
Ancient Greece
The Ancient Maya
Mesopotamia

Index

About the Author

Award-winning historian Don Nardo specializes in the ancient world and has published numerous books about the histories, mythologies, arts, sciences, and everyday lives of the Greeks, Romans, Egyptians, Persians, and other ancient peoples. He lives with his wife, Christine, in Massachusetts.